I'M POSITIVE!

Program Your Thoughts and Feelings to Create a Positive Life

MICHELLE ROBINSON

Bach. Counseling, Dip. Clinical Hypnosis, B.A. Dip. Ed.
Academy of Spiritual Practice

I'M POSITIVE!

Program Your Thoughts and Feelings to Create a Positive Life

MICHELLE ROBINSON

Director and Principal – The Academy of Spiritual Practice

B.A., Dip. ED., Bach. Couns., Cert Past Life and Soul Regression, Dip. CH.

Mind Potential Publishing
by *The Potentialist*

Copyright © 2021 Michelle Robinson and Academy of Spiritual Practice.

ALL RIGHTS RESERVED. No part of this book may be reproduced or transmitted in any form whatsoever, electronic, or mechanical, including photocopying, recording, or by any informational storage or retrieval system without the expressed written permission from the author and publisher.

Author: Michelle Robinson
Title: I'm Positive!
ISBN Paperback: 978-1-922380-42-5
ISBN Kindle: 978-1-922380-44-9

 A catalogue record for this book is available from the National Library of Australia

Category: Self Help Techniques | Mind and Body

Publisher: Mind Potential Publishing
Division of Mind Design Centre Pty Ltd,
PO Box 6094, Maroochydore BC
Queensland, Australia, 4558.
International Phone: +61 405 138 567
Australia Phone: 1300 664 544
Publisher: www.mindpotentialpublishing.com

Author: www.trustyourintuition.com
www.academyofspiritualpractice.com

Cover design by: www.ngirldesign.com.au

LIMITS OF LIABILITY | DISCLAIMER OF WARRANTY: The author and publisher of this book have used their best efforts in preparing this material and they disclaim any warranties, (expressed or implied) for any particular purpose. The information presented in this publication is compiled from sources believed to be accurate at the time of printing, however the publisher assumes no responsibility for omissions or errors. The author and publisher shall not be held liable for any loss or other damages, including, but not limited to incidental, consequential, or any other.

This publication is not intended to replace or substitute medical or professional advice, the author and publisher disclaim any liability, loss or risk incurred as a direct or indirect consequence of the use of any content.

Mind Potential Publishing bears no responsibility for the accuracy of the information provided as either online or offline links contained in this publication. The use of links to websites does not constitute an endorsement by the publisher. The publisher assumes no liability for content or opinion expressed by the author. Opinions expressed by the Author do not represent the opinion of Mind Potential Publishing or Mind Design Centre Pty Ltd.

Printed in Australia

CONTENTS

Foreword	1
The Mind-Body Connection	3
Red Flags That Signal Unhealthy Thinking	7
The ART of Positive Thinking	11
Emotions and Thoughts - The Chicken and Egg Mystery	15
Who Is Driving Your Bus?	19
Become Your Own Coach	25
Make It Your Choice	31
Release Judgment	37
Stay Present	41
Gratitude Is The Attitude	47
Assess Values And Beliefs	51
Steer Towards Happiness	55
A Little Help with Letting Go	59
Peeling The Emotional Onion	61
Find Your Voice	65
Grief	73
Releasing Anxiety	77
The G.R.A.C.E Process For Releasing Anxiety	85
Super-Charge Your Brain Training	91

The Power of Mental Rehearsal	95
Train With Tapping	99
Facing The Mirror	103
The Inner Control Room	107
A Final Word	113
Case Study: Judy's Story	114
Further Reading	117
Meet the Author	118
Further Books, Products and Courses by Michelle Robinson	119

FOREWORD

This book does not provide advice for any mental or physical health issue. It supports you in taking conscious steps to reprogram your thoughts and emotions towards choosing a positive approach to life.

You *can* re-train your brain and let go of old destructive habits and beliefs, whether you have formed them yourself or found them imposed on you by someone else. Life is not predictable and sometimes we can't choose what happens to us, yet how we respond to challenges, setbacks, successes and joys, is under our influence.

The strategies offered in this book to release unhelpful thoughts and feelings require your active involvement. They have been compiled from working in private practice in counseling and hypnotherapy over a fifteen-year period. A dedicated approach will bring the strongest benefits, yet each activity is straightforward and able to be completed in the quiet time you have available to yourself.

Please seek advice from a medical practitioner if you are experiencing very low mood, high anxiety or any thoughts of self-harm. This book is no substitute for required professional treatment.

You can download (or play online) 6 complimentary audios that support the activities in this book from web address:
https://bit.ly/impositivebook

Michelle Robinson

"You are what you think."

THE MIND-BODY CONNECTION

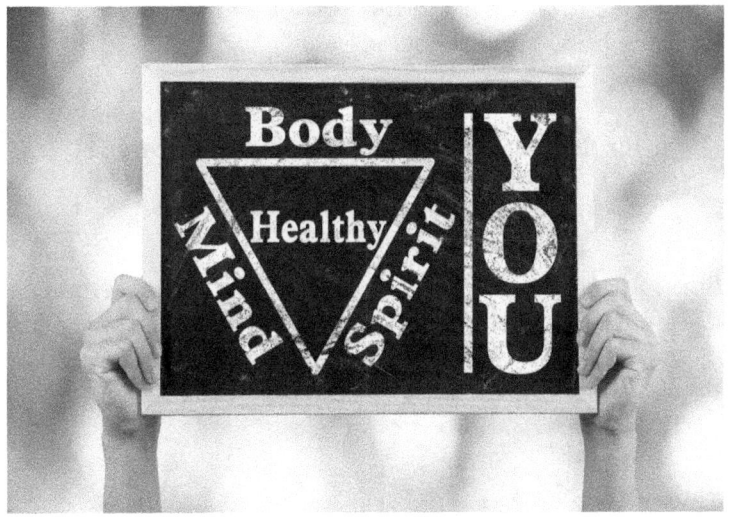

The importance of the mind-body connection in creating health is well documented by ancient cultures as well as contemporary authors. Today this idea is often expressed in the simple statement,

"You are what you think."

It is tempting to dismiss this concept, because it sounds too easy to say, perhaps even a little condescending, if spoken by someone offering advice. However, the key message of this book is that who we become *does* significantly depend on what we think.

Neuroscience now understands that our thoughts and emotions guide the creation of our neural pathways. Neural pathways are like the circuits or road-maps in our brain that drive our behavior, beliefs and habits.

Our thoughts and emotions guide the creation of our neural pathways.

Strong thoughts and emotions, especially if experienced frequently, create long lasting neural pathways that guide us towards responding in the same or similar ways each time. This means it is easy to continually repeat emotional and behavioral patterns from the past.

Familiar choices

If we are triggered to anger whenever we feel the world is unfair, then anger becomes an automatic response. If we practice tolerance because we choose to feel positive about others and our self, then this becomes our default. It is as though we follow a road that we have always taken, regardless of whether this helps or limits us. Other roads may be available that would suit us better, but we stick with familiar choices.

It is true that we cannot control everything that happens in our life; however, we *can* choose how to respond. We can learn to respond with flexible, positive behaviours and break limiting conditioning.

Inability to let go of past hurts, repeating unwise choices, feeling stuck in unhelpful habits, chronically low self-esteem, anxiety, anger and depression - these are some of our internal sign-posts that tell us unhelpful, automatic responses are running our life, and unfortunately, our health pays the price.

Very high levels of stress from repressed anger, guilt, grief, resentment, fatigue, anxiety, poor self-care and so on, harm us. They put pressure on our immune, autonomic and muscular skeletal systems, right down to cellular regeneration. Stressful emotions also compromise our emotional and mental health.

Positive emotions help us heal; they align us with well-being and optimism. They support cellular regeneration, a strong immune system, a healthy heart and the maintenance of a balanced physical, emotional and mental state.

This is easy to understand when we remember that each of us is an energetic being.

You are an energetic being

Although you appear solid, you are a swirling, flowing energy-mass comprised of billions of subatomic particles. There is far more space within you than matter, and so rather than aging in a fixed, predictable way, you evolve in every moment, renewing the cells in your organs, bones, blood, muscles and tissues.

You do this, even though you do not understand how. Below your awareness, a wise *inner healer* strives always to connect you with your blue-print for health.

You get to choose

You can support this process. By choosing positive thoughts, feelings, habits and beliefs, you create stronger health and a balanced perspective. This is the focus of the book.

Whether you are already practicing positivity or feel a call to make some changes, the information and strategies in the following pages are intended to help you create more self-awareness, flexibility of choices and well-being.

RED FLAGS THAT SIGNAL UNHEALTHY THINKING

Each of the following statements is a 'red flag' to alert you to sabotaging or unhelpful thoughts.

Reflect on whether any of these, or similar thoughts and feelings, influence your life.

Relationship with Myself

> I expect to fail at something before I begin.
> I dislike looking in the mirror.
> I have a critical voice in my head that keeps sabotaging me.
> I feel depressed, anxious, unable to get motivated.
> I have little self-confidence and self-worth.
> I feel guilty and blame myself for things that have happened.
> I feel lost and don't know how to feel happy.

Relationships with Others

> I am still very angry at one or more people from my past.
> I am self-conscious and embarrassed in social and work settings.
> I doubt whether my family/friends/partner really like or love me. Maybe they are just being polite/feel sorry for me.
> I give more to others than I receive. I often feel hurt and let down.
> I can't forgive myself for relationships that have failed.
> I find it hard to trust people and make new friends.

Repeated Patterns

> I can't believe how I keep making the same mistakes.
> I sabotage myself. I quit even when I want to do something.
> I befriend people who seem to need my help and I always end up hurt.
> I keep losing money/assets/relationships because of poor decisions or behavior.
> I sometimes put myself in harm's way and regret it later.
> I sabotage my relationships but can't seem to change.
> I sacrifice my well-being for others and then I feel resentful.

> I have an addiction or a habit I struggle to control.
> I stuff my feelings down. I can't express what matters to me.

You will notice that none of these statements expand your confidence or personal growth. The opposite is true.

Our decisions are generally based on what we are thinking and feeling, and then what we think and feel generally forms our beliefs.

Here is an example

If I think I am capable of performing a higher role at work and feel confident in my abilities, then I believe success is possible.

I also believe I am worthy of a promotion. I will take the steps required to apply for the role I desire.

If I tell myself that I am slow to learn new skills and feel like everyone else is smarter than I am, then I believe failure is likely. I am unwilling to apply for roles that might make me happier and believe I am destined to stay stuck in the same job.

Driving our decisions and habits

Our thoughts, feelings and beliefs interact below the level of our awareness to drive our decisions and habits. Just as unhelpful neural pathways are formed through repetitive thoughts, feelings and behaviors, our positive responses have been formed in the same way. Hence, choosing positivity is the gift we could wisely offer our self.

This requires training and time. Yet the results are worth it.

THE ART OF POSITIVE THINKING

No matter what goal we want to achieve, it is important that our unconscious mind and conscious mind work together to support success.

The automatic programs that store our habits, behaviors and beliefs sit in the unconscious mind, like software on a computer. Sometimes they are more like a virus or a version uploaded during childhood than currently helpful or relevant. Yet they continue to steer our life.

The activities and strategies in this book provide steps you can take to enhance and strengthen your positive thinking.

> **In summary, the ART of Positive Thinking involves:**
>
> › **Awareness** so that automatic, unhelpful thoughts and responses are acknowledged and changed before they impact you
> › **Resolving** or **Releasing** unhelpful emotions, beliefs and habits from the past
> › **Training** to choose positive responses rather than self-limiting habits and beliefs

Catching and changing any negative self-talk is important.

You will become a friend to yourself and not the saboteur.

Over time, a positive relationship with yourself becomes automated. You will not have to consciously choose to do the right thing for the rest of your life.

Healthy decisions will just occur naturally. You will no longer expect negative outcomes. You will become options-focused and open to possibilities. Life will feel like a learning experience and less like hard work or punishment. These are some of the internal shifts that occur with positive thinking.

You become the creator of your experiences, since how you respond feels more under your control. You recognize points of influence where you can shape outcomes.

In other words, positivity steers you away from reacting to life and towards creating your life.

With awareness, you learn to live in the present moment. You are mindful of what is relevant now and resist forming judgments or expectations based on the past. You free yourself from doing what you have always done. Every moment is treated as a fresh opportunity. This is very helpful for relationships, problem solving, decision making and keeping you grounded in what is real. If you experience anxiety, mindfulness is your friend.

Awareness

With awareness comes the realization that some old habits and beliefs need to be *released* because they only hold you back. Unhelpful feelings need to be *resolved* so you can move forward. You need to listen to yourself and honor what makes you happy. It is never too late to become the creator of your life.

To maintain a positive approach, you need to *train* yourself over time. You may have been criticized, abused or treated as though you are incapable of doing anything right. You may have low self-esteem, feel lethargic, anxious, depressed or angry. You may just feel 'stuck' in your life and want to move forward with more confidence and energy.

Don't give up. You deserve better than that.

EMOTIONS AND THOUGHTS - THE CHICKEN AND EGG MYSTERY

Creating a positive approach to life is not as simple as just changing our thoughts, because what we feel affects many decisions.

Do our feelings shape our thoughts, or is it the other way?

It is hard to know what comes first - whether our feelings shape what we think or whether our thoughts shape how we feel. This powerful *cause and effect cycle* works differently at different times; however, both thoughts and feelings need to be addressed in any inner work where you are seeking change.

Some people may say to you, *"Just think positively,"* as though the sun shines on their every moment. Their internal climate is favorable. They feel emotionally balanced and stable.

However, when you are anxious, depressed, stressed, grieving or frustrated it is difficult to feel motivated and positive. It is like your internal climate is mostly cloudy or stormy. Please seek help if you feel sustained sadness, lethargy or hopelessness, as a medical professional may be an important part of your recovery.

Like the weather, feelings can change.

On a positive note, there is something about our feelings we need to remember. Like the weather, they can change.

For example, imagine you are on a bus, feeling very nervous about a job interview in an hour's time. You feel shaky, nauseous and have an accelerated heart rate. Suddenly, the person next to you clutches their chest and collapses.

In this moment, your worry about the interview vanishes. You may feel anxious, but for a different reason. You quickly assess how to access help. The dread about the interview is rapidly replaced with the new focus of saving a life.

Here is another scenario:

> Imagine that you wake up feeling irritated by a thoughtless comment made by a colleague. It has bothered you during the night and you dread going to work.
>
> The phone rings and it is your best friend. They are distraught because their partner is having an affair and has left them. They need your immediate support.
>
> In this moment, are you still filled with resentment towards your colleague? Is your emotional focus the dread you feel about going to work?
>
> Most likely, the answer is "No."
>
> It is more likely that you feel a surge of energy and a flood of empathy and concern. Your mind may already be strategizing about how you can help your friend.

These examples show us that, like the weather, many of our feelings change moment to moment, depending on how we perceive and react to events.

Don't let unhelpful feelings entrench themselves and become your inner climate. Stay aware and pause before accepting your feelings as your reality. Take a deep breath, exhale and let unhelpful feelings pass through.

The Story of the Two Wolves

This is a commonly-told tale with a powerful message.

A small child is listening to her Grandfather. He tells her that within each person are two wolves. One is angry, selfish, mean and wants to hurt everyone. The second wolf is kind, patient, tolerant and loving. The wolves are always struggling with each other, each one desperate to gain control.

"Grandfather," exclaims the child in a worried voice, *"Which wolf will win?"*

Grandfather smiles and calmly responds:

"The one you feed."

Let's now examine strategies to help you feed the positive inner-wolf.

WHO IS DRIVING YOUR BUS?

If you imagine that your life is like travelling in a bus along the road towards your future, it is helpful to assess which aspect of you sits in the driver's seat.

Each of us is comprised of several aspects, some of which are highly functioning, capable and confident, yet most of us also contain childlike aspects that are fearful and inhibited. These less helpful aspects, in a misguided attempt at protection, may convince us that we are incapable of achieving what we want. They may suggest that we should never say what we really feel as it isn't 'good' or 'safe' to upset people. They limit our decisions, make us feel incompetent and may even convince us we do not deserve happiness.

When you are in touch with your higher functioning self, your perspective widens.

In particular, you understand that:

> - Every challenge has made you grow stronger. You are a survivor and know what matters in your life.
> - Life is like a school. You learn from your experiences and accept that it is pointless to punish yourself for past mistakes or regrets. You learn and move on.
> - You do not have to be perfect. No-one is. Your best is always good enough. Anyone who ever told you differently no longer controls you. Your life is your choice.
> - You do not have to please everyone. Being satisfied with yourself is what truly matters. No-one else can make you happy.
> - Life provides options. It's fine to explore as you go. You do not need to know the future. You can trust yourself to cope.

While the previous list is not exhaustive, you will understand that it is your highest functioning self who needs to have their hands on the steering wheel of your life. You do not want a fearful, childlike or limiting aspect to be in the driver's seat, yet sadly, they often are.

Activity 1

Step 1	At least daily, pause and assess which aspect of you is steering your life, making your decisions, or telling you what to think and feel. **Is the best and most appropriate aspect of you in control?**
Step 2	Mentally, connect with the strongest, wisest, most highly functioning aspect of yourself. Get a sense of what this aspect looks like and how she/he behaves, for example, her/his age, expression, tone of voice, achievements, goals, posture.
Step 3	Bring the *feeling* of that aspect forward in your mind, right to the front of your thoughts. Imagine this version of you taking their place in the driver's seat of your 'life-bus', with their hands on the wheel, looking ahead. Remind yourself that the best version of you competently guides your life.

Activity 2

Step 1	Take some time in a quiet place to reflect on the qualities and strengths you have developed from key experiences in your life. Bring them to mind one by one. Especially consider those experiences that led you to develop qualities such as courage, resilience, discernment, confidence, acceptance, forgiveness and compassion. Some of these memories will be joyful, while others may be less comfortable. Mentally, connect with the strongest, wisest, most highly functioning aspect of yourself. Get a sense of what this aspect looks like and how she/he behaves, for example, her/his age, expression, tone of voice, achievements, goals, posture. Do not revisit traumatic events or sad times. View all memories from a safe height or distance. Do not immerse yourself in old hurts. That is not the purpose of the activity. Your goal is to reflect on the learning gained.
Step 2	Ask, "What have I learned *about myself* from each of these experiences *that helps me move forward from here?*" Continue to ask the question, "And what else?" until you have a full list of your learnings.

Step 3	Re-write each learning in positive language so you can refer to it later.

For example, rather than, "I will never let myself be hurt like that again," you might write, "I will take care of myself and be careful who I trust."

Rather than, "It is pointless trying to please everyone," you might write, "I will honor myself and do what is right for me."

These statements reinforce positive thoughts and help create new neural pathways. Read them often. Sometimes, all we may have learned is to be more discerning about who we trust and that we are survivors. That's okay. Survival is a great achievement. It's a good basis from which to keep growing

This activity can be done in as many sittings as you need. Go gently. |

BECOME YOUR OWN COACH

Whose voice do you hear in your mind?

Many people listen only to their inner-critic. This is a voice that tells them they are worthless, fat, ugly or will fail. They are deaf to the wise voice within them that would encourage and support them.

If this sounds like you, then this chapter is important.

The critical, destructive voice may have belonged to an angry parent, sibling, teacher or partner, someone who bullied you or made you feel worthless. It was reinforced until it found a home in your mind. That critical voice has no place in your life.

You need to tune out negative self-talk and the voice of that inner-critic. While you tear yourself down and expect the worst, you continue to strengthen the unhelpful neural pathways.

From this point forward, find and listen to your inner-coach.

Your coach encourages and motivates you, keeps you on track and offers wise guidance.

This is a voice you can trust because it has your highest interests at heart. It keeps you moving forward with positive thoughts and feelings.

Be aware that you need to 'feed' and strengthen this inner-coach, so its voice is louder and clearer than the old critical voice that would see you fail. If you need to hear your coach as the voice of someone you admire - someone who inspires you that is fine. However, over time, allow this voice to become your own.

Your thoughts, your voice, your own coach.

There is an audio to support this activity.
Available from https://bit.ly/impositivebook

Activity 1

Step 1	If you are sabotaged by an unhelpful voice, reflect on where you hear this voice in your head. Does it speak to you from the front of your mind? The back? The left? The right? The middle? Allow yourself to know the direction its attack comes from.
Step 2	Identify who the voice belongs to and how long it has lived in your mind. Does the voice belong to one person, or is it a chorus of several voices who undermine you?
Step 3	Take responsibility for your part. Do your own doubts, fears or low self-esteem play a part in this criticism? Have you become your own saboteur because of past experiences or perceived failures? If the answer is "Yes," it is time to rid yourself of this unwanted intruder. Your thoughts are under your control. No-one thinks for you.

Step 4	Imagine that you have a dial in your mind that controls volume. You can use this dial to turn up or turn down the 'voice' of all thoughts.

Play around with changing the volume of the critical inner-voice. Whatever level it now sits on, turn it up so that it is even louder. Magnify the voice, just for a couple of seconds. It is under your control.

Because you can turn the voice up, you can also turn it down.

Turn down the volume of the critical voice until it is very quiet, until the dial is on its lowest possible setting. Experiment with moving the volume up and down. |
| **Step 5** | Have some fun with the sound of this critical voice.

For example, if it sounds authoritative, angry or sarcastic, switch the voice you hear to the voice of a cartoon character who sounds silly or whose temper is a joke. Hear it as a comical, quiet rant, rather than someone powerful and serious.

This step illustrates that you can control how you perceive your thoughts, even the voice of the inner-critic. |

Step 6	It is time to be rid of this intruder. Move the critical voice to the very back of your head, so far back you can hardly hear it, because it is so small and quiet. Shrink it and reduce the volume. Once you have achieved this, send it right out of your head altogether. Send it far away. It has no place in your life.

Activity 2

When you become aware of unhelpful thoughts or feel upset with yourself, do the following:

Step 1	Catch that thought or feeling; become aware of it. Be an observer and notice it. Don't be critical of yourself for having it. Say or think, for example: "There's that old thought again where I think I'm never good enough. I hear you in my head and I feel you making me shaky inside."
Step 2	Deny its power over you. Say or think, for example: "That's not who I am. You are a faded voice from my past. You are powerless to hurt me now."

Step 3	Imagine erasing the thought in the same way you close a computer screen. Do you want to save it? No! Delete it forever. You can also imagine squashing the thought in your hand and flicking it to the ground where you stomp on it. This is helpful if you feel frustrated.
Step 4	Replace that thought with three positive statements that counter the original thought. **For example:** "Every day I am learning to feel more confident. My best is always good enough. Eyes forward - the past is done." It is important that you choose the words that feel right for you when you practice this exercise.

MAKE IT YOUR CHOICE

This strategy is one of the essential keys to positive thinking.

A positive life means we take responsibility for our choices and actions.

Feeling as though we *must* or *should* do something is disempowering. It's like a cloak of effort sits on our shoulders before we even start.

However, when we *choose* to do something, the feeling is different. It's lighter. Our intention is empowered and energized.

Do you use words like:
- Must
- Should
- Have to or
- Need to

When you are thinking about a task?

Examples:

1. "I *should* go for a walk. I *must* get more exercise."

2. "I *must* do the housework this morning… I *have to* get it done before lunch."

Perhaps you also use the negative versions of these words?

Examples:

1. "I *mustn't* say what I'm feeling. It would only upset Mum."

2. "I *shouldn't* eat that dessert. I will never lose weight."

Whenever you find yourself thinking these kinds of phrases, stop and ask whether they are true.

Often, they are lies fed by an internal slave-driver who won't let you have fun or relax. The same is true for messages that use words like *always* and *never*.

Examples:

1. "I'll *never* be slim. I *always* put the weight straight back on."

2. " I *always* let myself down. I *never* follow through with anything."

There is no positivity in feeling as though we *must, should, have to* or *need to*, do anything. It's like someone else is telling us what to do.

Likewise, when our negative self-talk includes words like *always* and *never*, there is no room for change. We sabotage the possibility of improvement before we begin. These words often indicate that we have given up before we start or are unwilling to commit.

When we change a thought to make it *our choice*, we give it a positive rather than a negative perspective. We make ourselves aware of the benefits of the choice and release the weight of *having* to do it.

Examples:

1. "I have to go for a walk. I must get some exercise."

> **Change this thought to:**
>
> "I choose to go for a walk because I will feel energized and alert afterwards."

2. "I should do that office work now. It always builds up and gets out of control. I'll never get on top of it otherwise."

Change this thought to:

"I choose to do the office work today because it feels so good when it's done. I'll make a plan to get through it."

Choosing for our self, strips the blame and helplessness from our thoughts. It keeps us in touch with our inner-coach.

We can also choose to *not* do something. Not doing something may be the best option.

Example:

"I should visit Martha, but I don't really want to. All she does is gossip about everyone else. It wears me out."

Change this thought to:

"I choose not to visit Martha as I prefer to be around positive people who energize me."

Choosing to not engage with people or activities that threaten your positive mindset is empowering. If you do choose to help another person, do it willingly. What is offered with resentment is never a gift.

Activity

Are you forcing yourself to do something that you have told yourself is 'good for you' rather than *choosing* to do it?

- Reflect on the benefits of this activity and listen to your inner-coach. Take responsibility for choosing the positive path.

- Create three positive statements that remind you that your choice empowers this decision or activity.

Example:

Even though I enjoy my sleep, I choose to get up an hour earlier because I feel great after I have exercised. Every day it will get a little easier and I will feel better. I love having a flexible, stronger body.

Try to find a positive perspective, even when your choices are limited. The relief of accomplishment when a task is done is better than the dread of still needing to complete it.

RELEASE JUDGMENT

A judgment that leads to a 'that's good' or 'that's bad' mind-set limits our perspective. We miss all the possibilities that exist between these extremes. The phrase 'narrow minded' suits someone who is quick to judge based on their prejudices, habits or beliefs.

Whenever you find yourself about to criticize someone, ask: "Whose business am I in?"

The only adult's life we are responsible for is our own. Focusing on other people's dramas can be an effective distraction, but it does not create a positive life.

Becoming upset by another person's choices is like taking our money from a bank and burning it. Money symbolizes the energy and time we throw away when we get wrapped up in other people's business. Many are addicted to this habit and wonder why they feel exhausted so much of the time.

In judging and criticizing others, we deplete our own reserves.

> **Energy depleting behaviors include:**
> - *Gossiping. It's never harmless.*
> - *Resenting others for their beliefs, culture, sexual preferences and so on*
> - *Feeling envious or jealous of another person's life*
> - *Wanting someone else to change so we can be happier*
> - *Wanting to solve another person's problems for them*
> - *Expecting someone else to do what we want*
> - *Trying to control the lives of our adult children/ partners/ parents etc*
> - *Judging our friends/children/partners/siblings/ colleagues etc*
> - *Badgering others to agree with our point of view*
> - *Abusing, belittling, humiliating, or manipulating others*

Activity 1

> Next time you are about to judge someone, try saying to yourself, "That's an interesting point of view."
>
> Take a step back and be the objective observer. Unless they are breaking the law, everyone has a right to live the life of their choice.
>
> Remind yourself that you cannot know everything that has recently happened for that person. Everyone has a back-story. No-one is perfect. Take a deep breath and let irritation go. Should you choose to express what you feel, avoid lapsing into old language patterns that escalate an argument.

Activity 2

Look for the *intention* behind actions rather than judging the *outcomes*.

This is helpful for life in general, especially close relationships. Was the intention to hurt, anger or irritate you?

> *Find tolerance even when someone does something unfathomable, like cutting you off in traffic. Would they have chosen to make such a mistake? It's unlikely.*

> *You might practice saying something like, "Wow! That was a close call! I bet that gave them a scare." This creates far less stress than exploding with anger.*

> *It is also helpful to apply this principle of assessing intentions to yourself. Did you intend to cause hurt or harm? If not, then do not judge yourself too harshly. Above all, gift yourself kindness.*

> *It is healthy to self-reflect and make different choices going forward but wallowing in guilt keeps us stuck in the past. Guilt and shame steer us away from happiness and towards misery. They persuade us that life is full of shadows, when in fact, the light is right there waiting for us to step into it.*

> *Do not be your harshest judge; instead, be a trusted friend. Forgive yourself and learn from what you feel were mistakes. The passage of years often changes our perspective of events that seemed difficult or 'wrong' at the time.*

> *Relax into each day and enjoy the freedom that comes from disowning blame and guilt.*

STAY PRESENT

Staying present means that we remain focused on what is happening now, rather than wasting our energy obsessing about the past or the future.

Two of the largest contributors to anxiety are regret about unchangeable events in the past and worry about possible events that have not yet occurred.

Our strongest point of influence is always the present moment. In the present moment we are able to make decisions and adopt attitudes that will prepare us to face whatever the future brings.

Our best preparation for the future is to live well now.

Remaining calm and mindful in the current moment creates an inner resilience that stays with us as the present becomes the past and the future becomes the now.

Anticipating and dreading what *might* happen wastes our valuable energy and time.

We cannot control every event that happens to us, nor can we make another person love, appreciate or remain close to us. Life does not come with guarantees for an easy journey.

However, when we approach life as a learning experience, we accept that some pain, struggle and grief are inevitable. We learn more about who we are and find a level of acceptance. Acceptance does not change the past or future, but it can change how we respond. It guides us to acknowledge, process, and release pain so that we can move forward.

Remember that within each of us is the inner-coach. Your inner-coach has the WOW Factor - the voice of the Wise

One Within. The Wise One is calming, reassuring, realistic, motivating and encouraging. Even in its silence, there is peace.

Sometimes, our cluttered, hurried or fearful minds create too much noise for the voice and presence of our inner-coach to be heard or felt. It is as though static is destroying the connection to our best radio station.

You can change this by bringing your attention back to the present moment, affirming that you will cope with whatever life brings you, and gently breathing yourself into a calm state.

Activity

Meditation – Surrender and Focus

This activity is helpful for releasing concerns we have no control over and taking positive steps to manage issues under our influence.

Step 1	Sit or lie quietly in a place where you will not be disturbed.
	Allow your mind to scan your body, and consciously relax any muscles that are tight or tense. Use some deeper, slow breaths as you imagine the breath moving into the muscles, oxygenating and revitalizing them.
	Take your time. Check that your forehead, jaw, throat, shoulders, hands and abdomen are relaxed, as we often carry tension there. Breathe any stress away.

Step 2	Become aware of the issues and relationships that are on your mind, in particular those that concern, preoccupy or worry you. Allow them to arise one at a time.
Step 3	Without judgment, notice whether each concern is relevant to the present moment, rehashes the past, or anticipates the future.
Step 4	Without judgment, notice whether each concern is under your influence or control, or whether it is not.
Step 5	Without judgment, notice whether each concern is your responsibility or whether you are involved in another adult's life.
Step 6	Mentally divide your concerns into two groups. Group One contains everything that is current, is your responsibility and is under your influence or control. Group Two contains all concerns (relationships, worries, memories, unhelpful feelings) that are past or future-based, are not your responsibility and/or are not under your influence or control.

Step 7	Bring all the concerns in Group Two to mind.
	Visualize or sense that there is an energy line that links each concern to you. The energy lines might resemble string, spider-webs, ropes or even energetic chains. You created them. Now you will let them go.
	Cut each energy line so its tie to you is released. One by one, see or sense each concern in Group Two floating out of your mind. Send each concern out of your mind and far away from you, perhaps into the universe for higher healing. Choose how you achieve this.
	Surrender each concern so that you have the energy and focus for the issues that require your attention.
	Take 3 deep breaths and affirm to yourself, "I let them all go. I choose to surrender them, because I can."
	Take another 3 deep breaths and affirm, "I am centered and calm."

 There is an audio to support this activity.
Available from https://bit.ly/impositivebook

STAY PRESENT

Step 8	Bring your focus to the concerns that are current, are your responsibility and are under your influence or control.

For each concern, brainstorm three positive steps you can take to shape the outcome. Include achievable time-frames. Think 'outside of the box'. Be creative.

A helpful question to ask is, "What else is possible here?"

When you have finished, take another 3 deep breaths and affirm, "I am confident and capable. I trust myself."

Add additional affirmations that come naturally to you. |
| **Step 9** | Slowly count from 1 to 5, in time with your breath. Become more alert with every number.

Stretch, have a drink of water and when you feel ready, continue with your day or evening. |
| **Step 10** | Create an action-plan that maps out your positive strategies and timelines.

Adjust the plan until you are satisfied that you will commit to the time-frames and actions you have chosen. It will evolve over time. Remain flexible. |

GRATITUDE IS THE ATTITUDE

There is grace in gratitude because anyone can feel it.

Life does not have to be perfect before we can find things to be thankful for. It might take effort to notice the beauty of a flowering weed struggling through a crack in the pavement. However, if we look, blessings surround us in spite of our pain.

Life does not have to be perfect before we can find things to be thankful for.

Gratitude is also a grace because it is easy to practice. Pessimists always welcome problems, but you can train yourself to notice the 'good'.

Be thankful if you have legs to walk, healthy eyes to read, food to eat, clothes to warm you, friends who love you. Be thankful if you have clean water to drink because almost nine hundred million people do not.

Gratitude frees you from the disappointment of expectation and the ties of attachment. You are free to give gratitude and need nothing in return.

The more we appreciate the beauty around us, the more the world seems a nicer place. Our list of blessings grows with every minute we live. As our hearts soften and open, we feel appreciation for everything.

We also begin to see that the exterior world reflects our world within. One image mirrors the other.

Valuable lessons are available if we think of life that way. A tree sending its roots up through a concrete path reminds us we can work through any obstacle if we have determination. A dilapidated house urges us to take better care of our health and our bodies. A sunflower casting its head to the sky shouts to our spirit, "Have faith. Keep trying. Don't give up!" When we are alert to the lessons reflected in the world around us, everything can be a source of gratitude because all things are our teacher.

Activity

This exercise highlights the blessings for which you can express gratitude.

> Expressing gratitude involves being consciously aware of the present moment. This is not as easy as it sounds, because we easily slip into automatic mode and forget that every second is a new gift from life.
>
> For just one day, express gratitude as often as you can.
>
> Thank people for small acts of kindness like a smile or a wish for your health. Notice beauty in nature, even if it is a tiny beetle or a blue sky. Give thanks for what you see, experience and have, and do not fret over what you lack.
>
> **After the first day, continue for a second day.**
>
> If you notice a positive shift in your own life through feeling more energy, joy or respect for others, you will want to continue expressing gratitude at every opportunity.

When this becomes a habit rather than a lesson, you will change people's lives in ways you could not have imagined. They will trust you and engage with you from their hearts.

In turn, they will share their new positivity with others. The ripple effect continues, changing lives in small but meaningful ways. And you started it.

ASSESS VALUES AND BELIEFS

It is easy to assume that our values and beliefs are our own; however too frequently we absorbed them when we were children and have never considered whether they are relevant or helpful.

Values and beliefs operate in the unconscious aspect of our mind, so we are generally unaware of their impacts.

Our values are what we 'stand for'- the principles that underlie our way of life and who we are. For example, supporting individuals who are unfairly treated reflects a value of fairness.

Our values are often influenced by our beliefs.

Our beliefs are what we hold to be 'true' for us. For example, some individuals believe eating meat is a form of animal exploitation, while others eat meat without this concern.

Values and beliefs are formed through our own experiences, and also through exposure to the values and beliefs of others.

Between the ages of one and seven, children are very impressionable. They easily believe what they are told verbally and non-verbally from authority figures such as parents, grandparents and teachers. After that time, reinforcement of those messages by authority figures or peers makes them stronger. Eventually, the messages may be assumed to be 'true', irrespective of truth. Some beliefs are like viruses in a computer, causing damage in the background, even though the computer still functions.

Examples:

- A child who is told they are no good, stupid, ugly or fat will easily develop into a teenager and then into an adult with low self-esteem. It becomes their belief that they are not as lovable, intelligent or attractive as others.
- A child who is told they are naughty if they do not eat all the food on their plate may battle obesity throughout life. Leaving food behind somehow makes them feel like a bad person. This is despite their logical understanding that excess food just passes through them as waste and adds to weight gain.
- A child who observes a parent working excessive hours may grow up believing that unless they are always working, they are lazy. This causes chronic stress and poor work-life balance. As a manager, this person has little empathy with their employees.
- A child who is told they were an accident and should never have been born may grow up feeling directionless and worthless. They may find it hard to commit to a goal or relationships, because deep down they do not feel worthy of happiness.
- A child who hears their parents ridiculing individuals or groups because of their culture, beliefs or sexual preferences may innocently accept their parents' values, creating prejudice that has no basis in their own experiences.

Activity

Step 1	Take time to evaluate the values and beliefs you hold about yourself and others. Do this in a quiet place and do not rush. **Consider:** 1. Their origin. Did you form these values and beliefs or were they imposed by someone else? Whose voice or voices do you hear? Are they based on your own life-experiences or have you absorbed them from the media, peers, partners, family members and so on? 2. Their relevance. Are your values and beliefs relevant to your current life? What will you keep or adapt to suit you better? What will you discard for a more positive life?
Step 2	Write your beliefs and values in positive language so that you can remind yourself what you stand for. This helps integrate them into your mind, emotions and life. Feel the power of this activity. It is not just a mental exercise. Phrases like, "I am," "I believe," and "I stand for," will help you get started.

This activity is empowering, especially if you have not previously had the freedom to shape the direction of your life.

STEER TOWARDS HAPPINESS

This is a simple and yet powerful strategy to help you navigate your life in a positive direction.

Being aware of thoughts and decisions allows us to shape them so they support, rather than undermine, us. We stop living as though we are on autopilot and take control of where we are heading.

Optimistic, options-focused thoughts lead us to empowering, positive decisions.

> *We stop living as though we are on autopilot and take control of where we are heading.*

Self-sabotaging, pessimistic thoughts lead us to limiting, constricted decisions.

For example, imagine it's Sunday and I have a free day. How will I respond?

Below are two possibilities, with very different outcomes.

A. "It's a beautiful, sunny day. There's so much I could do. I'll start with a swim and see what else pans out after that. I am going to enjoy myself."

B. "It feels like it will get hot today. Heat just makes me so tired. I can't be bothered doing anything. It never works out the way I want it anyway."

The thoughts in Example A will steer me towards enjoying fresh air, being invigorated and exploring what feels good.

The thoughts in Example B will convince me I'm too lethargic to do anything except stay home and feel sorry for myself. I will miss out on the energizing swim and all the enjoyable activities that could help me feel better.

Our thoughts, via our self-talk, influence our feelings, and our feelings influence the decisions we make or do not make. We steer our self towards our happiness or away from it, moment by moment.

The previous example is mapped out on the following diagram. Thoughts above the mid-line steer towards happiness, while the thoughts below the mid-line do not.

You may benefit from also considering your thoughts in this way.

Towards Happiness

Thoughts ➡	Decisions
I'll enjoy my free day	I'll have a swim and do more fun things.

Thoughts ➡	Decisions
It's too hot. I can't be bothered.	I'll just lie around and do nothing new.

Away From Happiness

Activity

On a daily basis, reflect on whether you are steering your life towards or away from happiness.

> Ask, "Is this thought/action steering me towards more of what I want or is it steering me away?"
>
> Always name the specific goal or feeling you desire to achieve, such as happiness, peace, a specific achievement, a skill, confidence and so on. Be mindful of what your sensations, thoughts and feelings tell you in response to this question. Do not ignore the subtle shifts in awareness that might occur. Listen to yourself carefully.

Apply the strategies you have learned in this book to change direction, one decision at a time. You have many tools to help you.

Remember that there may be multiple options rather than just one solution, so stay flexible. Begin with small steps.

Consistency counts. It programs your neural pathways towards a positive focus and hence will enhance your life.

A LITTLE HELP WITH LETTING GO

Being aware of our thoughts and thinking positively are key-stones in creating a contented life.

However, sometimes we cannot move forward until we acknowledge and resolve the emotions that keep us 'stuck'.

Einstein reportedly said that the definition of insanity is continuing to do the same thing and expecting a different result. Put simply, unless something changes, nothing can change.

Denying troubling emotions may dull the pain, but the pain is never eased or released. Resentment and depression often follow because deep down we know we have placed our well- being low on our priority list. We may fool others, but we cannot fool our self.

If we feel apathetic, depressed, sad, angry, guilty, ashamed or hopeless for an extended period, then something needs to change.

It is important to emphasize that feelings are not 'bad', even when they make us feel uncomfortable. They are signals that we need to listen, take action and resolve something.

Put simply, unless something changes, nothing can change.

PEELING THE EMOTIONAL ONION

Emotions are often more complicated than we realize. Within one experience, several feelings may be buried.

For example:

> Julie found fear of abandonment and low self-esteem buried within her anger.
> Remy discovered fear of being alone and guilt interwoven with his grief when his partner died.
> Sarah found anger and helplessness at the core of her depression. She had been made redundant after working for her firm for eight years.
> Paul discovered a lack of self-esteem, envy of his brother and distrust of his friends at the core of his anxiety. He never felt good enough.

The following activity provides you with insights about unhelpful feelings so that they can be resolved. Troubling feelings can be powerful motivators for change.

You may need to undertake the process several times if your 'emotional onion' is multi-layered, in other words, contains a range of feelings you need to work through. Go slowly, taking your time, without judgment. You are once more, the observer - the detective who is searching for clues so you can better understand and heal yourself. Maintain this positive focus.

Activity

Step 1	In a quiet place, relax your mind and body, and close your eyes. Identify one emotion that is foremost in your thoughts and life - the reason you are undertaking this activity.
Step 2	Just like an onion contains several layers leading to its core, so this emotion may have several layers of feelings hidden within it. Allow yourself to sense and move through each layer of feeling. Pause often as you explore, slowly moving through and then below each feeling as you become aware of it. Notice whether you discover feelings of which you have been unaware.

Step 3	Each time you become aware of a feeling, reflect on: › *The participants and situations involved* › *Its impacts. How it helps you (e.g. does it protect you from failure? Does it allow you to avoid your fears?) and what it costs you? (e.g. does it limit your life? Does it damage relationships?)* › *Whether you are prepared to let it go* › *What you need to let it go so you can move forward* › *How you can access what you need* › *Whether forgiveness of yourself or others would be helpful* › *What it would mean for you when the feeling is released or resolved. This provides your motivation for change.* › *Understanding yourself with an honest, compassionate perspective releases guilt, fosters acceptance and makes it easier to let go of pain.*
Step 4	With the insights you have gained, take the steps that lead you towards resolving troubling feelings. Seek help from a professional if you need support at any stage of the process.

The activities that follow in the section *'Find Your Voice'* may also assist.

FIND YOUR VOICE

Finding your voice is helpful whether you need to express yourself to someone who is living or to someone who has already died.

It is never too late to express what needs to be said if this helps you heal. The most important thing is that you *feel* your words, rather than just saying them.

You may choose to communicate with the recipient/s in person, by phone or by email.

However, whether they ever receive your words is less important than your courage in speaking from your heart.

It is still valid to communicate with someone as though they are present, even when they are not. Your life may have moved on, they may be too frail, or you may no longer wish to have any contact with them.

They may even have died by the time you are ready. Do not let death or any other reason stop you from saying what is in your heart.

Whether or not you believe in life after death, the process of expressing what you need to say is healing. You can allow yourself to move forward. That is your choice and under your control.

There is no correct way to express yourself, so be as creative as you like. The following activities offer some ideas for consideration.

Activity 1: The Stage

This activity is helpful for communicating with a person or persons who hurt you or had power over you. It is a safe means of telling them how you feel and sending them out of your life.

Step 1	Find a quiet place where you will be undisturbed. Take a few minutes to relax, using your breath to become calm. Imagine you are in a large hall with a stage at one end. The stage is surrounded by a shield of the strongest glass in the universe. Nothing can get through it. In this hall, you have the power to command that people from your life come forward onto the stage so you may speak with them. You are completely safe because they are walled in by strong, cosmic glass, and they enter and leave via a door at the rear of the stage. When they leave, they go back to where they came from. There is a strong spotlight shining onto the stage; you can see clearly. Take a seat somewhere in the hall where you feel comfortable.
Step 2	Call people onto the stage, individually or in a group. Address them. Let them know the impact of their behavior on you, how it made you feel, and that you will never let them hurt you again. Connect with your feelings; make it real.

FIND YOUR VOICE

Step 3	Beside you, find a pair of very special glasses. When you put these glasses on, you can see any lines of energy that still link you with the person/s on the stage. The energy lines might connect your hearts, your minds, your sexual centers or your emotional centers in the abdomen. This is energy that keeps you stuck and you want to release it. If you sense energy ties between you, destroy them so that you break free from all mind games, mental abuse, sexual ties and emotional manipulation. You may choose to cut them, burn them, pull them out of you - do what you need to do. Whatever tools are required to help you, are right there.
Step 4	When you have finished, send the person/s away via the back stage-door, and spend some time relaxing before bringing yourself to full wakefulness. A nice warm shower during which you imagine you are being filled with positive energy is a good way to conclude this activity.

 There is an audio to support this activity.
Available from https://bit.ly/impositivebook

Activity 2: The Sanctuary

This activity helps you communicate with someone you deeply love and trust. The person may be alive or have already left their human life. Completed during a meditation, this guided visualisation allows you to speak from an open heart.

Step 1	Find a place where you can be undisturbed and use your breath to bring yourself into a relaxed, calm state. Mentally count down from 10 to 1, and as you do so, imagine coming down a flight of stairs that has a special door at the bottom. Every step relaxes you deeper into your own mind and deeper into comfort. The special door leads you directly into your sanctuary. This is a beautiful place where you feel safe, calm and comfortable. Take some time to create your sanctuary. Use all your senses to make it real. Notice that there is a spot where two or more people can sit comfortably and talk. Your sanctuary might be a place in nature, an idyllic creation of your mind, a room in your own home - there are no limitations. Only those people you invite may enter your sanctuary. It is protected from all but those you love and trust.

Step 2	Once you are settled in your sanctuary, invite the person or persons you wish to share time with to join you. They will find a natural doorway that allows them to enter - create this door for them if you like. Speak from the heart and enjoy this special time. Allow your emotions to flow. Your inner sanctuary is always available to you – it is a refuge from stress and difficult times. Notice everything about it so you remember it well.
Step 3	When you are ready, thank your guests and watch them leave. Find the door through which you entered and come back up the ten steps. Every step brings you closer to full wakefulness. By 10, you are awake and alert. Take some time to relax and reflect on your experience.

 **There is an audio to support this activity.**
Available from https://bit.ly/impositivebook

Activity 3: The Fire Ceremony

This activity allows you to release a variety of unhelpful thoughts, habits and feelings. Spiritually, this ceremony is often conducted as close as possible to a full moon.

Step 1

This ceremony is about you. Consider carefully what you choose to release from your life. You will need a small fire or flame for this activity and a series of release-statements written on individual pieces of paper.

You cannot release another person from anything in their life, but you can *release yourself* from ties with them. You can address them directly and let them know how you feel.

Your statements should also include what will replace each thing you give up. There are many ways to write release-statements. A few examples follow:

1. "I choose to release the habit of procrastination. I am committed to taking positive action in my life. I promise myself I will enrol in the nursing program next year."
2. "I release my addictions to sugar and binge eating. From this point forward, I will nurture my body with healthy food. I am learning to respect myself more every day."
3. I hereby release myself from all emotional ties with Mark. I am free to move forward. We are done. Done. Done! I open myself to loving and respectful relationships."
4. "Dad - I have been deeply hurt by your lack of love, but I choose now to release this hurt, because I can. I forgive the ignorance that made you unable to show love. I feel sorry for you because you missed out on loving me. I am worthy of love and do not need your approval to be happy. I am me, Dad, and that's good enough."

Step 2	When you are ready, find a safe, private place where you have access to a small fire or flame. A campfire provides a nice atmosphere, but a candle flame will suffice.
Step 3	One by one, read your statements aloud and then burn them in the fire. Watch as they are consumed, and affirm to yourself, "It is done now. I am free." Choose the words that feel right for you. You could also perform a fire ceremony with a friend or friends in a shared experience. The ceremony releases all you do not wish to keep and offers positive affirmations to carry you forward. It is better to have fewer, strongly felt release-statements than a long list in which some are less significant. **Remember to be fire-safe and careful.**

GRIEF

It is important to talk about grief.

Grief has many faces. These include sadness, anger, lethargy, guilt, regret, frustration, loss and abandonment. It often involves a sense of sadness and loss for someone or something taken from our lives. We may have had no choice in that.

Many life events can trigger grief.

It may follow the death of someone we deeply care for, even if that relationship was complex or conflicted. It may come when a much-loved pet passes away.

Grief results when we are separated from treasured relationships with our children, grandchildren, spouses/partners, other family members and friends. Family breakdowns cause intense grief when access to loved ones is restricted or denied. In cases of acrimonious separations, parents, grandparents and siblings may feel this loss as keenly as if their loved ones had died.

Grief may also accompany the loss of employment.

This can especially happen if the loss was unjust, undesired or the result of ill-health. The shock and financial stress of unemployment can create problems such as depression, anxiety and confusion about our self-worth. Many people's identity is tied to what they do, and when they can no longer 'do' that, there is a large void within.

Serious ill-health is a common trigger for grief.

We feel disconnected from who we once were, and vulnerable to life's uncertainties. Ill-health highlights the weakening of abilities and strengths we could once rely on. The future seems overwhelming and unknown.

If you are grieving, honor your feelings and acknowledge any limitations you are experiencing. Grieving is a natural process and will affect each of us at some time in our lives.

Acknowledge what cannot be changed, and do not try to hurry through the healing process. Above all, remind yourself that your life matters, and that you owe it to the life you were gifted at birth to continue living as positively as you can. Grief is not a life-sentence for sadness. The loss may always remain, and yet you can choose to live your life the best way you can and bring the best of you to what life you have left.

Please seek professional help if your grief is prolonged, feels too painful to bear or prevents you from leading a satisfied life. With time and the right support, the feelings of grief do lessen, and a positive life can continue.

RELEASING ANXIETY

The first thing you need to know if you struggle with the symptoms of anxiety is that you are not a weak person and anxious thoughts do not mean you are going insane.

You need to release any shame or guilt that you are carrying because of how anxiety makes you feel. You also need to believe you can recover.

It may be difficult for those around you who have never experienced anxiety to understand you. Your decisions, feelings and behaviors seem foreign to them. This analogy of foreignness is a good one. It is like your lives are ruled by two completely different political systems. Their bodies and minds allow them the freedoms of a democracy. They can choose what they want to do, feel, believe and think. In the democratic 'map' of their life, they are willing to tackle new challenges, take some safe risks, explore new opportunities and trust their ability to stay safe. They think you are the same as them - or should be.

What they may not know is that your body and mind have you 'locked down', as though you live in an army-state. Even though at some stage you were the ruler of this state, your generals have decided that life could not be trusted, that you are not safe, and so for your own protection they have taken control. For your own well-being, you no longer have the freedom to explore new opportunities or take safe risks. You are strongly urged to stay within designated safety zones and infringements bring a rapid and arresting response of fear. The irony is, the protective mechanisms that developed to look after you are shrinking your life and making you miserable.

This is not easy for others to understand, especially when you seem just as capable as they are. To you, however, it seems like your life and their lives are worlds apart.

When you understand the message behind this analogy, you can glimpse your way forward to recovery from anxiety. Fighting against yourself leads only to more pain. Your best strategy is to re-learn that you are wise, competent and can be trusted to make the decisions in your life.

The demands of what may currently seem like powerful generals are actually more like the cries of a defiant child who is desperate to get your attention. Changing your perspective of anxiety's sensations takes away much of their power. Your thoughts and reactions to your body's defence-mechanisms play a crucial role in whether you are 'ruled by generals', or whether you 'disarm a screaming toddler'. Your perceptions of your experiences create your world.

Stress and Anxiety

There is a popular misconception that *anxiety* is just another word for *stress*. However, anyone who experiences anxiety knows this is not true.

The symptoms of stress are familiar to most of us. Stress is a natural response to challenges that demand our decisive action or problem solving. When we feel swamped by competing priorities, under pressure to complete a task or are juggling limited finances, stress is a likely response. Some stress gears us up to take required action; however, its usefulness, depends on its intensity.

While a little stress might motivate us in a positive way, high levels of stress are both harmful and unhelpful. Too much stress hampers efficiency and impairs decision-making. There are also serious health risks that accompany prolonged or intense stress. Creating a balanced life-style is essential for longevity and well-being.

In contrast to stress, anxiety is a pervading feeling of dread and/or fear with accompanying physical sensations.

Anxiety creates a compelling belief that something terrible is about to occur and its sensations may mimic a serious health episode, like a heart attack. Despite the fact there is no credible threat to our safety, our bodies and minds behave as if our annihilation is imminent. Somehow, this makes our feelings all the more frightening, because we do not understand their origin or cause.

Anxiety also plants intrusive, scary thoughts that grow like weeds in our mind. In the same way an incoming tide swallows the beach, anxiety creeps into spaces where logic lived only moments previously. It can make a competent person fear they are losing their mind or are about to die. Yet paradoxically, this person is completely safe, sane and well.

While stress and anxiety are not the same condition, very high levels of stress can cause anxiety. When an invisible tipping point is reached, some people flip from stress into anxiety or panic.

If you are experiencing anxiety, do not feel you are alone. Figures suggest that anxiety affects up to one in four people at any time.

You also need to remember that life is a journey. There are no right or wrong, pass or fail judgments required every time you attempt something new. It is okay to explore possibilities. You do not need to see the destination before you put a foot on the road.

Even as children, we grew from the consequences of our choices. It was the way life taught us to develop resilience and potential.

> *You can recover from anxiety and panic. You can reclaim your life.*

Most importantly, you need to know this; no amount of worry about what may happen will protect you from life's challenges. Life is what it is. Duality exists in sunshine and darkness, summer and winter, regeneration and decay, joy and sorrow. Safety precautions and avoidance strategies cannot protect you from what is inevitable. Experiencing life is why you are here.

As We Think, So We Create.

Our thoughts play a crucial role in whether the sensations of anxiety seize us in their grip or pass with minimal disturbance. How we think when confronted by our fight, flight or freeze sensations will either strengthen or short circuit them.

It is not the sensations that cause us to feel afraid; it is our perceptions of what these sensations mean and our emotional responses to them that generate the fear.

This concept is easily demonstrated. Whether I have just run a sprint race or am having an anxiety attack, I will have many similar sensations - a racing heart, tightness in the chest, shortness of breath, sweating, trembling legs, shakiness, perhaps even dizziness and nausea.

However, after a sprint race, I accept these sensations are natural; I can observe them without fear, knowing there is no threat to my well-being.

Once you learn to be unafraid of anxiety's sensations, you are on the road to recovery. Those sensations will diminish and possibly fade completely from your life. At the very least, you will acknowledge them when they occasionally arise and pay them little attention.

Panic Attacks

Sometimes the anxiety symptoms become overwhelming, resulting in a panic attack.

A panic attack involves a period of intense fear that develops abruptly, peaks within ten minutes and usually lessens within half an hour. The terms anxiety attack and panic attack are used interchangeably. A panic attack is an overload of fight and flight hormones caused by extreme anxiety.

As with all health conditions, please consult your medical practitioner if you believe you are experiencing panic attacks.

The first panic attack often occurs spontaneously.

You might have felt hot, sweaty, dizzy, weak, tight in the chest and detached from your body or your environment.

It is not surprising these sensations made you very afraid, especially if you did not know what caused them. You may have thought you were having a heart attack or a nervous breakdown.

Sometimes the trigger for a panic attack is obvious, particularly if you are confronted by your phobia. However, these panic attacks, though very disconcerting, are less likely to create as much distress as spontaneous panic attacks. Spontaneous panic attacks occur suddenly and unpredictably, often without a known cause.

If you experience spontaneous panic attacks you will likely remember a time in your life when the problem did not exist. Wondering where that rational, competent *you* has gone fuels your fearful thoughts. You may now have panic attacks in situations where you were previously relaxed, and be woken at night with a pounding heart and other anxious sensations. All of these experiences are common.

The truth about panic is this; provided you are in a safe environment and do not have complicating health conditions, the sensations of panic are not dangerous.

Panic tries to trick you into making assumptions about your state of mind and your health based on the intensity of how you feel.

However, how you feel does not represent reality.

> **Reflection:**
>
> To illustrate this point, reflect briefly on someone you know who is terrified during a horror movie. There is nothing real that can hurt them and yet they feel terrified. The screen's images may even haunt them long after the movie has ended.
>
> Now reflect on someone who could watch the same movie and enjoy the thrilling sensations, without any ill-effects. They know there is nothing dangerous or real about their feelings or the movie's images.

Our thoughts - through how we perceive, interpret and judge our world - play a major role in how we feel. The more we struggle against anxious sensations, the stronger they become. There is a saying, "What you resist, persists," and this is true of anxiety and panic.

You can change your perceptions of the sensations and strip them of fear. They are not the real you. Treat them like an unwelcome guest and tell yourself they will soon be gone.

THE G.R.A.C.E PROCESS FOR RELEASING ANXIETY

THE G.R.A.C.E PROCESS FOR RELEASING ANXIETY

Recovery from anxiety may not mean you will never feel those old sensations; however it does mean they will not distress you.

The sensations caused by your flight, fight or freeze responses mimic those of excitement, such as the nervousness of an athlete before a big competition. Keep reminding yourself of that.

Once you change your perception of anxious thoughts and detach from the sensations, anxiety has no reason to persist.

The G.R.A.C.E. process comprises five steps

This is a practical strategy you can implement immediately.

1. **G stands for Greet.** Greet the anxious sensations when they arise. They are not the real you, but rather are generated by a part of you that is like a misguided child or unwelcome guest with distracting behavior. *Greet* implies *acknowledgement*, with the underlying assumption that the sensations will soon be gone.

2. **R stands for Reality Check.** Bring yourself back to the present moment and check what is real. Nip flights of fantasy or imagined catastrophes in the bud.

3. **A stands for Accept.** You know the sensations of anxiety are caused by adrenaline and other chemicals triggered by your fight, flight or freeze responses. Shaking, shivering, feeling sick - all those sensations - are just your body trying to process the stress chemicals you have created. They will soon pass. You are safe and sane. Hang in.
4. **C stands for Centered and Calm.** Use the B.E.T. Relaxation Routine to stay centered and calm in any situation. An explanation of the B.E.T. follows.
5. **E stands for Engage in life.** The final stage is to immerse yourself in something which takes your attention away from any remaining anxious sensations.

The B.E.T. Relaxation Routine

This is a relaxation routine that helps lower anxiety through the use of breath and cue words or phrases. Pressing the tips of two fingers against your thumb strengthens the relaxation response over time.

B = Body

E = Emotions

T = Thoughts

Step One

On a scale of 1 to 10, where 10 is the highest possible level of anxiety, rate your current level of anxiety.

Step Two

Lightly press the tips of two fingers and the thumb together on one hand and hold them like this while you practice the B.E.T. Routine.

Step Three

Relax Your Body.

Take three or more deep, relaxing breaths (in to the slow count of four and out to the slow count of six) as you relax all the muscles in your body. Be aware of physical relaxation moving through you as you take these deep breaths.

Think the cue word, "Relax."

Step Four

Relax Your Emotions.

Take three or more deep, relaxing breaths (in to the slow count of four and out to the slow count of six) as you exhale any troubling feelings or emotion. Blow them away like smoke.

Think the cue phrase "Let them all go."

Step Five

Relax Your Thoughts.

Take three or more deep, relaxing breaths (in to the slow count of four and out to the slow count of six) as you allow your thoughts to relax. Bring yourself to the present moment and to what is actually 'real.'

Think the cue phrase, "I'm centered and calm."

> Alter the cue phrases to suit your preference; however, maintain consistency.
> Work through three rounds of the B.E.T. Routine, and then re-assess your anxiety levels.
> Practicing this routine reinforces your relaxation response. In time, you may effortlessly think your cue words, "Relax. Let them all go. I'm centered and calm," and feel calm in any situation.

 There is an audio to support this activity.
Available from https://bit.ly/impositivebook

SUPER-CHARGE YOUR BRAIN TRAINING

Throughout this book, we have explored strategies to create a positive life.

To recap, some keys to a positive life include:

- Being aware of our thoughts and changing those that sabotage us.
- Allowing the highest functioning aspect of our self to steer us towards our goals and desires.
- Tuning in to our inner-coach for guidance.
- Remaining flexible and options-focused. Most challenges have more than one solution.
- Understanding that we are responsible for our lives and others are responsible for theirs. Stay within 'our business'.
- Staying grounded in the present moment. Conserve energy by not wasting it obsessing the past or future.
- Remaining an objective observer, free of judgment.
- Offering understanding and kindness to our self and others.
- Surrendering concern for situations and relationships that are not under our influence or control.
- Accepting what cannot be changed and moving forward.
- Being true and authentic. No-one else can live our life or be us.
- Freeing our self from the need for approval from others.

- Clarifying the beliefs and values we stand for.
- Working through emotions that have limited us or kept us stuck.
- Seeking help from a medical practitioner or other expert if we have powerful or lingering feelings that interfere with us living a satisfying life.

You can further empower a positive life by adding some specific brain training activities to your day.

Consistent and regular practice over at least a three-month period will create long term, automatic neural pathways. If you do not persist for at least three months, the helpful neural pathways may break down when you face a situation that has triggered unhelpful thinking or behavior in the past. This places you at risk of a return to the older habits. A range of targeted brain training strategies follow.

THE POWER OF MENTAL REHEARSAL

Training the brain requires repetition and commitment.

Our imagination is our ally in brain training because our unconscious mind finds it hard to distinguish between reality and fiction, especially when we are focused on something. For example, we may cry in a sad movie, despite knowing the plot and characters are fictitious.

Video-games produce a similarly compelling response, firing up chemicals that signal excitement and danger, even though we are playing in a simulated world.

One of the strongest habits for success, therefore, is to mentally rehearse an outcome, *as if we have already achieved it.*

When we imagine success, using all our senses, our unconscious mind creates the expectation this will occur. New neural pathways then develop to support our success.

Mental rehearsal is excellent for a wide variety of purposes such as an impending job interview, an exam, a task that has several steps, refining a skill, planning a strategy and completing a project. Committed men and women in a wide range of industries including athletics, dance, sports, politics, sales, law, business, racing, pilot-training and many others use mental rehearsal to improve their performance.

Activity

This activity can be completed in just a few minutes. It is particularly helpful before you go to sleep at night or as you begin a new day.

Step 1	Make yourself comfortable and close your eyes. Bring to mind a specific goal or activity. While your goal may involve a need for your high performance, it could also be as straightforward as staying calm and confident in a challenging meeting.
Step 2	Mentally rehearse this activity, seeing each aspect unfolding in the best way possible. Focus on each 'thing' you do that brings about the success. Do this by imagining you are watching yourself on the screen of your mind. Notice what you did to ensure the activity went well. Of course, in life you can control only the part that is under your influence. However, in mental rehearsal, create the best scenario possible.
Step 3	Complete the same mental process *while looking through your own eyes*, so that you experience yourself 'doing' rather than 'watching'. Rehearse the ideal scenario as if you are really there. Make it as real as you can, using your senses of sight, hearing, touch, smell, taste and so on. Feel what this achievement means to you. This is a powerful brain training method. Practicing it is worthwhile. Train your brain to expect success and utilize this strategy as often as you can.

TRAIN WITH TAPPING

Train With Tapping

The purpose of tapping is to interrupt thoughts and feelings that are troubling you. You will deny that they belong to you and strip them of their power. Once the troubling thoughts and feelings are interrupted, you will replace them with positive statements that reinforce your goal.

You can also tap solely to reinforce positive statements.

The example below offers a process for interrupting self-sabotaging thoughts about quitting an exercise program. The method could be adapted to a wide range of situations.

In your tapping practice, use language that feels natural to you.

Step One

Tap two fingers gently above your top lip (under your nose) as you describe and name what you are thinking and feeling.

For example:

"There it is again, that thought I should quit my gym class because it feels too hard...that I should give up my exercise program because I never stick to anything. It makes me feel anxious in my stomach and weak in my mind. That's not who I am. That's not who I choose to be. That's just outdated wiring in my brain."

Step Two

Tap gently with the same two fingers just below your bottom lip, (in the crease above your chin bone), as you let that thought and feeling go.

For example:

"I will not quit this time. I let that fear go. I let those sabotaging thoughts go. They're just the echoes of old, weak wiring in my brain. Already those thoughts are fading and will soon be gone. The past is done!"

Take 3 deep breaths and blow unhelpful thoughts and feelings away, like smoke.

Step Three

Now tap the karate point on one hand. The karate point is about half way along the outer edge of your palm under your little finger. Make strong positive statements that change any sabotaging thoughts or uncomfortable feelings, tapping as you do so.

For example:

"Every day I feel more committed to my self- care. I choose to be healthy and fit for life. I choose that for me. I easily stick to my exercise plan. My gym program is my choice. I love a fit, healthy body. I create my life and I love the life I create. I feel stronger and more positive in every way... committed...calm. I am ready to do this."

Take another three deep breaths to clear your mind and enjoy your day.

You will find many versions and examples of tapping, also called Emotional Freedom Technique, on YouTube and the internet. It is a therapy in its own right, and you may enjoy researching it further.

FACING THE MIRROR

Mirror-work is a powerful brain training technique. It reinforces the positive statements we most need to hear. These positive statements are called Mind Rehearsal Statements because they train the mind to choose positive thinking as a default.

When we look into the eyes of our reflection, we connect with our inner-self. There is an honesty there that we cannot hide from.

Complete mirror-work by speaking aloud, if your environment permits. The vibration of your voices adds extra power. However, take as many opportunities as you can during the day or evening to connect with yourself in this way, whether speaking aloud or in your thoughts.

Create Mind Rehearsal Statements that fill you with positive inner-resources and feelings.

If this activity feels challenging, allow yourself to know that you are *learning* to appreciate, value and respect yourself. You are learning to create a positive life. All learning takes time and practice. That is perfectly okay.

Activity

Step One

Create one or more positive Mind Rehearsal Statements which you will reinforce while looking into a mirror.

> Here are a few examples of Mind Rehearsal Statements to get you started.
>
> 1. "I am learning to respect myself. I am learning to like who I am."
>
> 2. "I am learning to feel more positive each day. I choose to create a positive life."
>
> 3. "I am worthy of love and respect. I am worthy of a loving partner. I am worthy of deep, true, love."
>
> 4. "I feel confident at work today. My best is always good enough."

Step Two

Sit or stand in front of a mirror and close your eyes. Take a few deeper breaths, as you allow your body, thoughts and feelings to relax. Like watching the waters on a lake become calm at sunset, feel yourself becoming centered. When you are ready, open your eyes.

Step Three

- *Gaze at your reflection with a soft, gentle, focus. Some anxiety may be natural if you have disliked mirrors in the past.*
- *Take a moment to feel connected to the 'inner-you', whose natural orientation is towards a healthy, positive life. Place one hand on your heart.*

> Continue to look into the mirror as you speak your statements. Do this now.

Step Four

> Close the activity by taking a few deep breaths, feeling energized and alert.
> Mirror-work reinforces the programing of your mind towards positive thoughts and feelings.
> Completing your most important statements in front of the mirror each day strengthens your connection to a positive life.

THE INNER CONTROL ROOM

Another version of mind rehearsal, the Inner Control Room activity quickly and effectively programs you towards a positive day.

Repetition and using your imagination as vividly as possible empower your success.

The Inner Control Room is a space you create within your unconscious mind where you take control of your physical, emotional and mental responses.

When you consider how your body heals itself and keeps all the autonomic processes, like your heart-beat working every moment of your life, it is obvious that your unconscious ability to create well-being is huge.

In your Control Room is a Control Panel from which you can tune-up your thoughts and feelings to create a positive day. On this Control Panel you can turn on switches that link you to resources you need, such as motivation, or turn off resources you don't need, like addictive behaviors or panic. You can also adjust dials and/or swipe-pads to strengthen behaviors and feelings that you would like to increase, or to turn down behaviors and feelings that are not helpful.

There is a large, comfortable chair in front of your Control Panel.

You can visualize your Control Room and Control Panel in a way that feels right for you. Some people imagine the Control Room like a pilot's cockpit, with the Control Panel surrounding them. Others create a Control Room and

Control Panel with the special 'powers' of a video-game. It is your choice.

Possibilities
- › Switches are helpful for turning behaviors and feelings on and off.
- › Dials and swipe-pads are helpful for increasing and decreasing feelings, motivation and resources.

The following suggestions may spark some ideas to help you create your Control Panel:

1. A range of switches to turn off cravings or addictions e.g. to alcohol, nicotine, other drugs, sugar, fatty-food, obsessive thoughts or behaviors
2. A switch to turn off panic
3. A switch to turn off self-sabotage
4. A switch to turn off negative thinking
5. A switch to turn off anger
6. A switch to turn off procrastination
7. A switch to turn on positive thinking
8. A switch to turn on staying-power
9. Dials and/or swipe-pads to increase or decrease feelings, resources and skills e.g. inner strength, motivation, self-care, self-confidence, patience, determination, commitment, courage, energy, restful sleep.

Make the dials or swipe pads specific to a purpose.
For example:

- Commitment to Healthy Eating
- Motivation to Walk Every Day
- Patience with my Children
- Confidence at Work
- Inspiration for my Writing
- Accuracy with my Tennis Serves

The settings may range from Low to High or be adjusted with numbers e.g. from 1 to 10.

Decide what is controlled with a switch, a dial or a swipe-pad. There is no right or wrong way to create your control panel.

 There is an audio to support this activity.
Available from https://bit.ly/impositivebook

Activity

Step 1	Set a clear intention for the tune-up.
	Take a few moments to mentally create the Control Panel within your Inner Control Room. Be creative and make it as real as you can.
	Imagine a label under each of the switches, dials/swipe-pads. Ensure they are relevant to the tune-up you want to achieve. You can add or delete items any time.
	What adjustments on your Control Panel will support the outcomes you have chosen today?

Step 2	Find a place where you can be undisturbed, and use your breath to bring yourself into a relaxed, calm state. Allow every muscle in your body to release tension as you drift deeper within your own mind. Take your time. Disconnect from any unsettling thoughts. Surrender them for now.
Step 3	Mentally count down from 15 to 1, and as you do so, imagine coming down a long, winding staircase that has a door at the bottom. Lightly tap the index finger on one hand as you come down each step. Every step relaxes you deeper into your own mind and deeper into comfort. Behind the door is your Control Room and inside is your Control Panel with the large chair in front of it. Your imagination can add any other helpful items it chooses.
Step 4	Open the door, enter the Control Room and take your seat. Imagine or sense the switches, dials and/or swipe-pads on your Control Panel. What adjustments on your Control Panel will support the outcomes that you have chosen today? It may be that you need to adjust only one or a few mechanisms to set them at optimum levels. Perhaps, a larger tune-up is required. You will know. Take a few moments to assess the current settings on your Control Panel.

Step 5	Having checked the settings on the relevant mechanisms, make all the adjustments required, one by one. Complete this as if you are looking through your own eyes. If you can't visualize the Control Panel, just sense that you are making the adjustments. That's okay. With each adjustment, mentally reinforce the change with a brief affirmation. **Examples:** - *"Anxiety - pulled back from a 7 to a 2. Locked in."* - *"The Panic Switch is off!"* - *"Motivation to walk - 10 out of 10. Great."* - *"Patience with my children - maximum strength."* Have some fun. Your imaginative involvement is the key to your success.
Step 6	When you have made all your adjustments and are happy with their new settings, leave your Control Room and slowly walk back up the steps. With every step you return towards your waking state, and by the time you reach step 15, (the top of the staircase), you are completely awake and alert. Stretch, have a glass of water and enjoy the rest of your day or evening.

A FINAL WORD

The strategies in this book support you in creating a positive attitude for life. They also assist the reprograming of your unconscious mind to develop helpful neural pathways which reinforce, rather than undermine, your goals.

Once we have awoken the potential within us, we realize that we have the power to shape our lives. We choose to respond flexibly, intelligently and with current insights to life's challenges and joys. Old automatic responses that once limited us, fade away. We do not feel like victims; rather we are empowered to live to our potential. We are comfortable learning as we go and are kind to our self; we do not need to be perfect nor rely on others to validate our worth.

This is the journey you are undertaking. Good luck. You can do it. I'm positive!

Blessings,

Michelle Robinson

CASE STUDY: JUDY'S STORY

Judy Smith was in trouble. For several years she had been living with an autoimmune illness that caused intense pain, fatigue, and such stiffness in her legs that she could hardly walk.

I watched Judy as she struggled to hobble the small distance from her car to my clinic room for her appointments, and my heart ached for her.

Judy was stuck on the roundabout of specialists' consultations, conflicting diagnoses and strong medications. Nothing seemed to offer a long-term solution.

In Judy's sessions, we worked on strengthening what she had some control over in her life. We focused on the decisions over which she had influence. In addition to hypnosis that programmed her towards her own inner-healing, I worked extensively in other ways. Each session we discovered reasons for gratitude. I called them the 'chinks of light' that sparkled in her life, even if they seemed hard to see at times. We discussed strategies that would help her focus on the positive aspects of her life. She learned that she could control how she responded to her challenges.

CASE STUDY: JUDY'S STORY

Judy has tremendous courage and she was determined to get well.

She worked with every strategy I offered, giving 100% commitment to living a positive life.

Over time, her condition began to improve. Even more than that, Judy became lighter in spirit. She discovered a connection to her own inner-spirit and her spiritual guidance.

The strategies, information and activities in *'I'm Positive!'* helped Judy turn the lights back on in her life. Today, she is a different woman from the one I met almost seven years ago. She chooses to have a positive outlook on life. She chooses how she responds to people and lets unhelpful thoughts go. It was hard, but she has learned to let other people's negativity or judgments bother her less. She is generous and kind, but she also knows now how to look after herself and when to conserve her energy. Judy's story was one of my motivations for writing this book. She found it helpful, and my hope is that you will too.

> **Judy says:**
>
> *"When I first met Michelle, I was in a bad way, physically, emotionally and mentally. With her skills, knowledge and caring nature, she enabled me to turn my life around. I still use many of her strategies in my everyday life. The positive life-skills she shared with me have enabled me to survive with my health issues, and I have learned how to cope and live a much better life."*
>
> Judy Smith, Hervey Bay, Australia

FURTHER READING

Chopra, Deepak and Rudolf E Tanzi. *Unleashing the Explosive Power of Your Mind to Maximize Health, Happiness, and Spiritual Well-Being.* New York, Random House, 2012.

DisPenza, Joe. *Breaking the Habit of Bring Yourself: How to Lose Your Mind and Create a New One.* Carlsbad, Hay House 2012.

Doidge, Norman. *The Brain That Changes Itself: Stories of Personal Triumph from the Frontiers of Brain Science.* New York. Penguin Group, 2007.

Leaf, Caroline. *Switch On Your Brain: The Key to Peak Happiness, Thinking and Health.* Grand Rapids, Baker Books, 2015

Pillay, Srinivasan S. *Life Unlocked: 7 Revolutionary Lessons to Overcome Fear.* New York, Rodale Books, 2010

Shapiro, Francine, PhD. *Getting Past your Past: Take Control of Your Life with Self-Help Techniques from EMDR Therapy,* Rodale, New York, 2012

Wilde, Maggie. Unleashed: *How to Embrace Who You Are and Empower Yourself to Reach Your Potential - FAST!* Black Card Books, Stouffville, Canada

MEET THE AUTHOR

Michelle Robinson

B.A., Dip. Ed, B. Counseling, Dip. Clinical Hypnosis, Cert. Soul Regression.

Michelle is a qualified teacher who has more than twenty years' experience teaching adults and teenagers. She also has a degree in counseling and is a qualified clinical hypnotherapist. Her passion is to help people who feel disconnected from their lives find their inner strengths, connect with their life and enjoy the freedom of personal choice.

Michelle is a published author. Other works include:

'Your Intuitive Gifts At Work. From Passion to Profession. The 8 Keys to Excellence in Spiritual Practice.'

'Karma Couples. A Spiritual Self-Help Guide For Troubled Karmic Relationships.'

Find Michelle's books in print and eBook format on Amazon, Kindle and other publishing platforms.

Email: Michelle: michelle@academyofspiritualpractice.com

FURTHER BOOKS, PRODUCTS AND COURSES BY MICHELLE ROBINSON

'Your Intuitive Gifts At Work' will propel you toward excellence in working with your intuitive gifts. Inside you will find 8 Master Keys. These Keys reveal how to fine-tune your skills and master your spiritual connections so that your gifts reach their full potential. The keys give you the structure and guidance to transform your Passion to your Profession. Whether you help others as a psychic, a medium, a healer or in any aligned field, understanding the principles and steps required to launch an inspired Intuitive Practice sets you on the road to success.

Available from www.trustyourintuition.com/shop-now

'Karma Couples' helps you make sense of confusing and troubled relationships with a partner. As souls, we incarnated to Earth for human experiences, and these experiences were designed to help us grow. That does not mean we have to stay stuck in an unhappy relationship or leave with a broken heart.

Can you stay, or is it time to leave? The choice is yours, but make that choice without the burden of pain, blame and guilt. Assess your relationship with new eyes and an open heart.

This book includes access to 8 complimentary MP3 audios to guide you through the meditation activities in this book.

Available from www.trustyourintuition.com/shop-now

FURTHER BOOKS, PRODUCTS AND COURSES BY MICHELLE ROBINSON

I'm Positive! helps you let go of unhelpful thought patterns, emotional hurt and outdated beliefs so you feel confident, optimistic and in control of your choices. If you have been undermining your own achievements or impacted by the negativity of others, this book shows you how to steer your life in the right direction.

Program your mind so that positive thoughts and feelings are your natural default.

This book includes 6 complimentary MP3 audios to guide you through some of the activities in the book.

Available from www.trustyourintuition.com/shop-now)

STUDY ONLINE WITH BY MICHELLE ROBINSON

The Certificate in Advanced Intuitive Practice

This flexibly delivered, 9 module online program helps you propel your intuitive gifts to their highest potential.

Eight Keys to Excellence guide you towards establishing best practice in using your intuitive gifts, whether you work with psychic skills, evidential mediumship, trance mediumship or spiritual healing.

You will learn strategies to create the confidence and courage to step up and work with your gifts. If using your intuitive gifts is your passion, you will receive the skills and knowledge to transform that passion into your profession.

During this program you will connect with your soul's calling and develop closer relationships with your spiritual guides. You will also receive practical strategies and tips to guide you to set up and market your own intuitive practice.

This program helps you find the balance between living a human life, which is important, and fulfilling your soul's reasons for incarnating in this life.

This program is approved by the International Institute of Complementary Therapists (IICT).

Completing the requirements of this program will make you eligible to join the International Institute of Complementary Therapists as a practitioner in Psychic Skills and Mediumship/Channeling. Having joined IICT, you would then be eligible to apply for insurance in these modalities with their approved insurer.

Email: Michelle for more information:
michelle@academyofspiritualpractice.com

Enrol Now:
https://www.yourintuitivegiftsatwork.com/advancedcourse

Or go to:
www.trustyourintuiton.com/shop-now

CARD DECKS BY MICHELLE ROBINSON

Daily Compass Oracle Cards

This deck unites the wisdom of Spirit with positive messages for everyday life.

I have worked with thousands of people whose lack of self-confidence sabotages them from living their best lives. They feel too anxious or unworthy to find the happiness they deserve. Yet, when communicating with Spirit, I am consistently in awe of the great love and encouragement our Spiritual Guides and Loved Ones offer us. They never want us to give up on ourselves. Their encouragement is conveyed in these cards.

The 'Daily Compass' helps you navigate your life with greater clarity and confidence. The cards are uplifting and practical, suitable for all levels of experience.

www.trustyourintuition.com/shop-now

Open to Spirit Oracle Cards

This stunning deck offers insights of encouragement and hope. Its beautiful imagery and messages take you on an inward journey, away from the hectic physical world.

Many people live busy and ungrounded lives. Their mind is so overwhelmed that their Soul feels unheard amid the demands of daily life. This deck listens to the calling of your Soul. It provides gentle spiritual nourishment, offering wisdom that is deeper than a standard, psychic message.

Whether your chosen cards provide insights about your intuitive gifts, your soul's calling, self-healing or messages from the Spirit World, you will feel uplifted, supported and loved.

www.trustyourintuition.com/shop-now

www.ingramcontent.com/pod-product-compliance
Lightning Source LLC
Chambersburg PA
CBHW071519080526
44588CB00011B/1487